WORLD CUP RIVALS

ALGERIA VS. EGYPT

by Jules Allen

CAPSTONE PRESS
a capstone imprint

Published by Spark, an imprint of Capstone
1710 Roe Crest Drive, North Mankato, Minnesota 56003
capstonepub.com

Library of Congress Cataloging-in-Publication Data is available on the Library of Congress website.
ISBN: 9781666357455 (hardcover)
ISBN: 9781666357462 (ebook PDF)

Summary: The national soccer teams of Algeria and Egypt have a rivalry spanning decades. What made the teams fierce competitors? How are both country's fans involved in keeping this rivalry going? Easy-to-read text and fantastic images describe famous matches and star players.

Editorial Credits
Editor: Erika L. Shores; Designer: Dina Her; Media Researchers: Jo Miller and Pam Mitsakos; Production Specialist: Tori Abraham

Image Credits
Alamy: Foto Arena LTDA, 13, 25, REUTERS, 9; Getty Images: Clive Mason, 11, KHALED DESOUKI, 5, 21, 23, 28, picture alliance, 26, Wavebreakmedia Ltd, 15; Shutterstock: Adil_Designs, Cover, (right), Aleena_4, Cover, (left), BERMIX STUDIO, 7, Celso Pupo, 12, GIROMIN STUDIO, 19, IconiaGh, 20, kckate16, Cover, 1, (Egypt flag), Lightboxx, 14, mohsen nabil, 29, (both), Per Bengtsson, 16, T.Lesia, Cover, 1, (Algeria flag), tuulijumala, Cover, (lights), vectorlaboratory, Cover, 1, (ball), wavebreakmedia, 18, winui, Cover, (pitch)

Design elements:
Shutterstock: huangyailah488, Ursa Major

All internet sites appearing in back matter were available and accurate when this book was sent to press.

Printed and bound in the USA. PO 6034

TABLE OF CONTENTS

Fighting for a Chance at the Cup............4

Fierce Rivals 10

Winning at AFCON 20

Rival Stars...................................... 24

The Rivalry Continues........................ 28

Glossary.................................. 30

Read More............................... 31

Internet Sites........................... 31

Index 32

About the Author 32

Words in BOLD are in the glossary.

FIGHTING FOR A CHANCE AT THE CUP

Egypt and Algeria's men's national soccer teams faced off. They were playing for a spot in the 2010 World Cup. An Egyptian player got the ball. Fans cheered! He ran it down the **pitch**. He took a shot on goal. Missed!

Egypt got the ball back. Emad Moteab took the **cross**. He ran it toward the goal. Score!

Algeria's Nadir Belhadj (left) and Egypt's Ahmed Elmohamady (right)

The World Cup happens every four years. National soccer teams play in **qualifying** tournaments. They add up points from matches. Now Egypt and Algeria were tied. They had to play another match. The winner would go to the World Cup.

The next match was heated. Algeria made a shot on goal at 40 minutes. Antar Yahia let it bounce. Then he fired it in. Score!

Algeria won 1–0. They would go to the World Cup. Egypt's team and fans were upset. They said fighting made the match unfair. Algeria's team bus had been attacked before the match. Three players were hurt.

Algeria's Antar Yahia (left)

FIERCE RIVALS

Egypt and Algeria are **rivals**. Fans of rival teams have strong feelings. The media plays up these feelings. Sometimes rival fans and players fight at matches.

FACT

Algeria has been to the World Cup four times. Egypt has been there three times.

Egypt and Algeria's rivalry goes way back. Fans are loyal to their teams.

Belgium (red) and Algeria (white), 2014 World Cup match

Egypt (white) and Russia (red), 2018 World Cup match

In 1934, Egypt was the first African country in the World Cup. They went in 1990 and 2018 too. Algeria played in the World Cup in 1982, 1986, 2010, and 2014.

A 1989 match pitted these countries against each other. Egypt and Algeria were playing for a spot in the 1990 World Cup. This match decided who got in.

Algeria was the better team at this time.
They needed one point to get to the Cup.

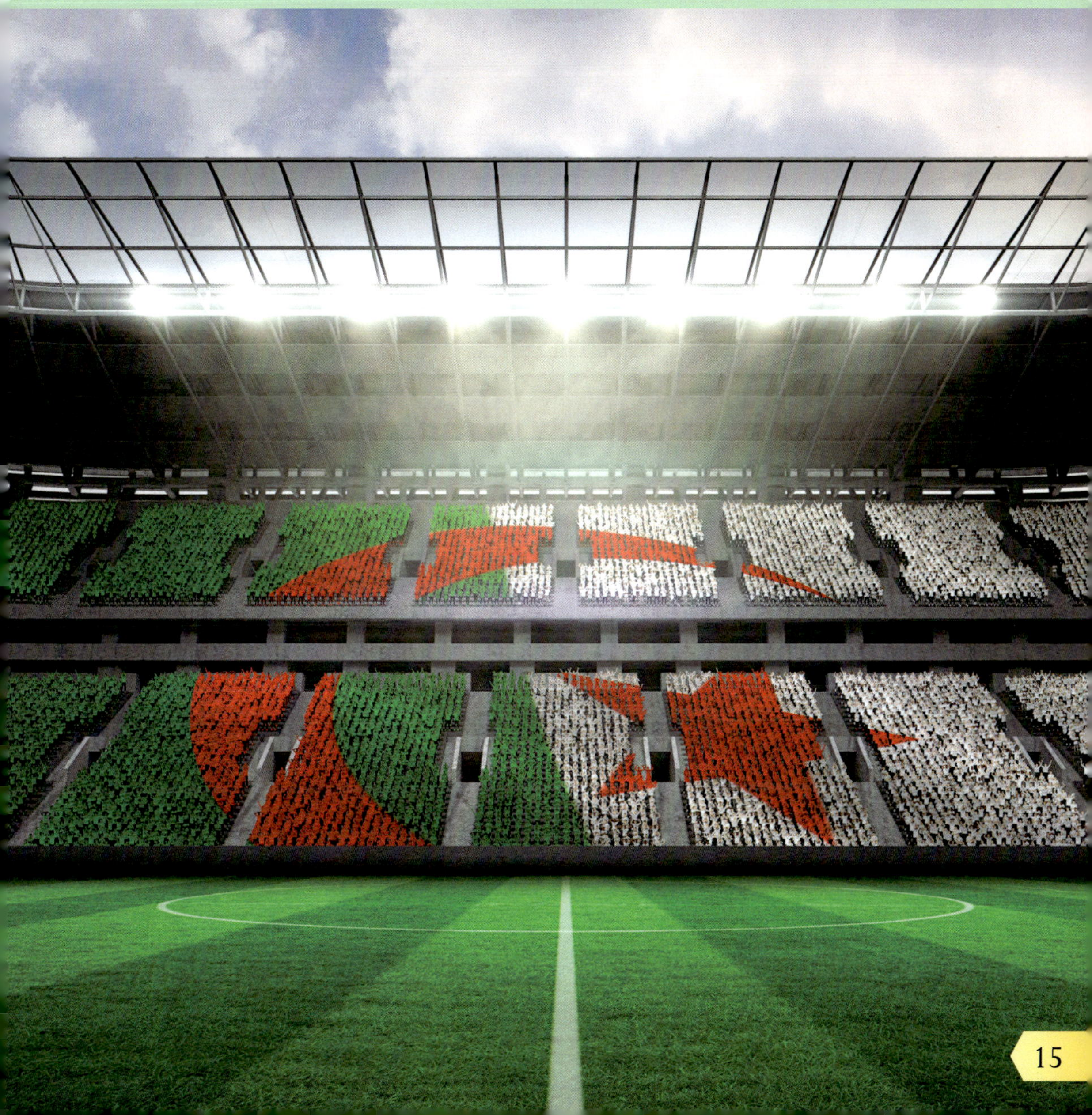

It was the fourth minute. An Egyptian player sent the ball out wide. Hossam Hassan got it. He was Egypt's all-time top scorer.

Hassan's shot floated to the goal. The goalie could not stop it. The ball hit the far side of the net. Score!

Egypt was up 1–0. The players battled hard. But neither team scored again. Egypt had their spot in the World Cup.

Algerian fans were upset. Many thought the referee made unfair calls. They said he had helped Egypt win. Both teams' fans fought after the match. An Algerian fan attacked an Egyptian player.

WINNING AT AFCON

Algeria and Egypt also compete at the Africa Cup of Nations, or AFCON, tournament. In 1990, Algeria beat Egypt 2–0 in an early round. Algeria later won the title.

FACT

The Africa Cup of Nations happens every two years.

Algeria's Karim Ziani (left) and Egypt's Emad Moteab (right), 2010 AFCON semifinal

Egypt won more starting in 2000. They won AFCON in 2006, 2008, and 2010.

In 2010, Egypt beat Algeria in the semifinals 4–0. They won the final. They were the first nation to win three AFCON titles in a row.

FACT

Egypt's team name is the Pharaohs. Algeria is called the Desert Foxes.

Egypt's Emad Moteab (left) and Algeria's Rafik Halliche (right), 2010 AFCON semifinal

RIVAL STARS

Both teams have had great star players. Mohamed "Mo" Salah is one of the best players in the world. He helped Egypt reach the AFCON final in 2017.

Salah scored five goals in qualifying for the 2018 World Cup. One was a **penalty shot**. He helped Egypt get to the World Cup.

Lakhdar Belloumi

Lakhdar Belloumi is the best Algerian player of all time. He holds the record for most **caps** for Algeria. In 1982, he scored against West Germany at the World Cup. It was the winning goal.

Belloumi started the "blind pass." A player looks in one direction. That player then kicks the ball in the other direction.

THE RIVALRY CONTINUES

Egypt and Algeria keep competing. Fans love their teams as much as ever. They remember matches of the past.

Qualifying matches are always exciting. Fans root for their team to go to the World Cup. Fans look forward to more great matches.

VIVA LALGERIE
1933

GLOSSARY

cap (KAP)—an appearance in an international match for a national team

cross (KROSS)—a pass in from the wings that can result in a shot on goal

penalty shot (PEN-uhl-tee SHOT)—when a player takes a turn shooting off against the goalie

pitch (PICH)—the field a soccer match is played on

qualifying (KWAL-i-fy-ing)—a stage in which competitors try to win entry into an event

rival (RYE-val)—someone or something that tries to defeat or be more successful than another

READ MORE

Hellebuyck, Adam, and Laura Deimel. *FIFA World Cup.* Ann Arbor, MI: Cherry Lake Publishing, 2020.

Jökulsson, Illugi. *Stars of World Soccer.* New York: Abbeville Press Publishers, 2020.

Shaabneh, Nevien. *Mohamed Salah: Get to Know the Soccer Superstar*. North Mankato, MN: Capstone Press, 2020.

INTERNET SITES

Algeria
espn.com/soccer/team/_/id/624/algeria

Egypt
espn.com/soccer/team/_/id/2620/egypt

FIFA World Cup Facts for Kids
kids.kiddle.co/FIFA_World_Cup

INDEX

1982 World Cup, 27
1990 World Cup, 14, 15, 18
2010 World Cup, 4, 8
2014 World Cup, 13
2018 World Cup, 24

Africa Cup of Nations (AFCON) tournament, 20, 22, 24

Belloumi, Lakhdar, 27

fans, 4, 8, 10, 12, 19, 28
fighting, 8, 10, 19

Hassan, Hossam, 17

Moteab, Emad, 4, 23

qualifying tournaments, 7, 24, 28

Salah, Mohamed, 24

World Cup appearances, 4, 8, 10, 13, 18, 24

Yahia, Antar, 8, 9

ABOUT THE AUTHOR

Jules Allen is a children's book editor and author who lives in Minneapolis. She loves sports, art, all kinds of books, and small dogs.